How to Make a
Paper Airplane

by Robin Raymer

Harcourt

Orlando   Boston   Dallas   Chicago   San Diego

Visit *The Learning Site!*

www.harcourtschool.com

MRS. MOP'S TOY SHOP

OPEN

Airplane Kits

FUN WITH
HIEROGLYPHS

Peter wants an exciting new toy. He likes the
cranes and the cats with ears that twitch.
"Please, can we go into Mrs. Mop's Toy
Shop?" he asks.

"Let's go home and make a new toy," says Mom. "This book tells how to make paper airplanes."

You can make paper airplanes, too.
Here is what you will need.

- Blank paper 8-1/2 inches wide and 11 inches long
- Small paper clips
- Tape

These tips will help you.
- Read the directions carefully.
- Follow the steps in order.
- Use the pictures to help you.
- Make each fold nice and sharp.
- Ask for help if you need it.

Step 1

Fold your paper in half the long way. Lay the folded paper on the table. The fold should be at the bottom. The dotted lines show where folds are.

before

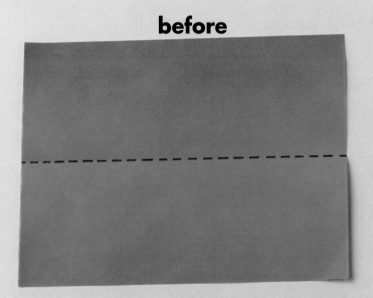

after

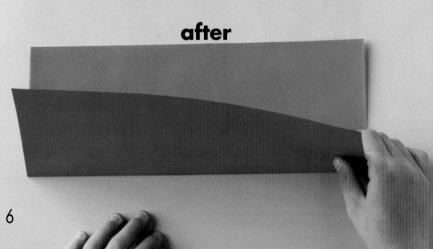

Step 2

Take the top left corner of the paper. Fold it down to your first fold. Make a triangle like the one in the picture. Line up the bottom of the triangle with your first fold.

before

after

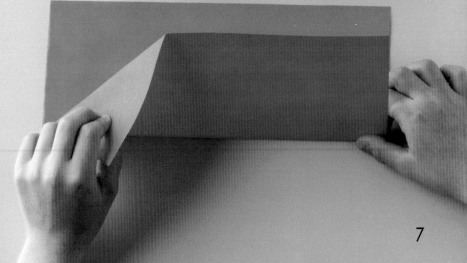

Step 3

Fold the paper down again. Make another triangle. The new triangle will be longer and thinner. Its top point will bend to the right. Line up the bottom of the triangle with the bottom of the paper.

before

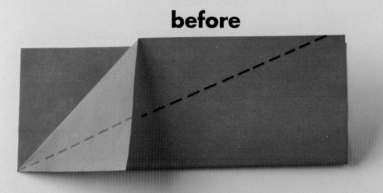

after

Step 4

Make another triangle. Do this by folding the paper down again. This triangle will be even longer and thinner. It will look like an arrow pointing left. Line up the bottom of the triangle with the bottom of the paper.

before

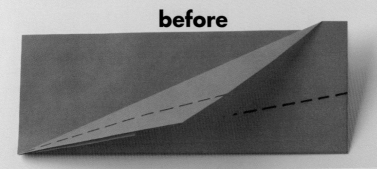

after

Step 5

Flip your paper over so the fold is at the bottom.

before

after

Step 6

Take the top right corner of the paper. Fold it down to the bottom fold. Make a triangle like the one in the picture. Line up the bottom of the triangle with the bottom of the paper.

before

after

Step 7

Fold the paper down again. Make another triangle. The new triangle will be longer and thinner. Its top point will bend to the left. Line up the bottom of the triangle with the bottom of the paper.

before

after

Step 8

Make another triangle. Do this by folding the paper down again. This triangle will be even longer and thinner. It will look like an arrow pointing right. Line up the bottom of the triangle with the bottom of the paper.

before

after

Step 9

Now open your plane so it looks like the picture. Use a small paper clip to hold the bottom of the plane together. Put the paper clip about one or two inches from the plane's nose. Put some tape on the top of the plane to hold the wings together.

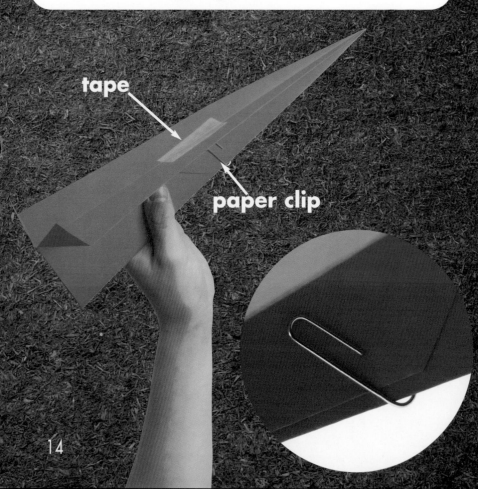

tape

paper clip

Flying Your Plane

To make your plane stay up longer, fly it up into the wind. If you see it twitch or nose-dive, don't worry. Bend its tail up. You can also move the clip or take it off.

Peter's Mom says, "Promise not to fly your plane inside the house!"

"OK!" says Peter.

How to Make a
Paper Airplane

Follow these
steps to begin ▶

To find out more about paper airplanes,
you can
- look in library books.
- look in children's magazines.
- visit children's websites.